UniCoRn PuzzLes

Stella Maidment and Daniela Dogliani

Editor: Alexandra Koken
Designer: Elaine Wilkinson

Copyright © QED Publishing 2013

First published in the UK in 2013 by
QED Publishing
A Quarto Group company
230 City Road
London EC1V 2TT

www.qed-publishing.co.uk

A catalogue record for this book is available from the British Library.

ISBN 978 1 78171 140 8

Printed in China

If you get stuck,
the answers are
at the back of
the book!

2

Welcome to the land of the Unicorns!

This is Sparkle, the little unicorn.

And this is her Fairy Godmother.

Solve the puzzles in this book and help Sparkle find her way to the magical picnic.

Look out for Betty the butterfly too. You'll find her in every picture!

3

One day, Sparkle the little unicorn
gets an exciting invitation.
It's from her Fairy Godmother.

4

Look who's brought the invitation! Can you find his twin brother in the picture?

Come to my magical picnic by the river. Be ready for some surprises on the way!

Can you spot these things?

a mouse

a dragonfly

two red flowers

5

Sparkle likes picnics, and she loves surprises! To get to the river she needs to go through the Enchanted Forest.

Can you help Sparkle find the way to the forest?

6

Can you spot
these things?

three pine
cones

a frog

two
rabbits

Enchanted
Forest

7

All the little forest animals come out of their homes to say hello.

8

Can you find
five matching
pairs of animals?

Can you spot
these things?

a rainbow

a bird's nest

two
toadstools

9

Suddenly the tallest trees are covered with beautiful flowers!

Sparkle looks around in wonder.

One tree is different from the others. Can you see which one?

Can you spot these things?

Sparkle's Fairy Godmother

two white birds

three butterflies

11

Then, as Sparkle trots out of the forest, pretty butterflies fill the sky.

The butterflies are flying together to make a shape. Can you tell what shape it is?

Can you spot
these things?

a castle

two cottages

a mole

13

At last Sparkle reaches the river. The water is shallow and there are lots of stepping stones.

Can you spot these things?

a family of swans

14

a frog

two fish

Can you help Sparkle to find her way across the river?

Two handsome peacocks stand at the entrance to a field. "This way to the picnic, Sparkle!" they say.

PICNIC

16

Can you find four differences between the two peacocks?

Can you spot these things?

PICNIC a signpost

three paper lanterns

two paper windmills

17

"Welcome!" says Sparkle's Fairy Godmother. "Look, all your friends are here!"

Can you spot these things?

some bunting

a magic wand

two yellow balloons

Sparkle's best friend, Bluebell,
has a green and white mane.
Can you see her?

It's the best picnic ever!
The unicorns close their
eyes and wish for their
favourite food – then it
magically appears!

Can you spot these things?

a picnic basket

a loaf of bread

two pears

Sparkle wishes for her favourite food: cupcakes!
Which cupcake is different from the others?

What food would you wish for?

21

Next there's a magic rainbow slide, and fluffy clouds to bounce on.

Can you spot these things?

a tiny fairy

a squirrel

three blue flowers

22

Which unicorn is bouncing the highest?

In the evening, all the mother unicorns come to collect their children.

Can you match the mothers to their daughters?

Can you spot these things?

two rabbits

an owl

the moon

25

"I've had a wonderful time!" says Sparkle to her Fairy Godmother. "Thank you for all the surprises!"

26

Follow the ivy trails to find one more surprise for each little unicorn.

Can you spot these things?

three daisies

two ladybirds

a snail

Answers

Pages 4-5

The bird's twin brother is circled in red.

Pages 6-7

Follow the red line to the Enchanted Forest.

Pages 8-9

The red lines link the animal pairs.

Pages 10-11

The different tree is circled in red.

Pages 12-13

The butterflies have made a heart shape.

Pages 14-15

Follow the red line to cross the river.

Pages 16-17

The four differences are circled in red.

Pages 18-19

Bluebell is circled in red.

Answers

Pages 20-21

Betty

Pages 22-23

Betty

The different cupcake is circled in red. You can wish for anything you like!

Bluebell bounces the highest!

30

Pages 24-25

Betty

Follow the red lines to match the unicorn
mothers to their daughters.

Pages 26-27

Betty

Follow the colourful lines to lead each unicorn
to her present.

More unicorn fun

Unicorn picnic!

Make little unicorn horns out of circles of coloured card. Cut a slit in the centre of each circle and fold one side over the other to make a tall, thin cone. Tape it together, make two holes near the edge. Fix elastic through the holes. Pack a picnic basket and a rug and go for a picnic in the garden or to the local park. Make sure you take a grown-up with you.

Treasure hunt

Make some tiny horseshoe shapes out of coloured paper or card. Be sure to make lots! Then one person should hide some treasure – maybe some sweets or a little toy – and lay a trail of horseshoes to it. Finally, the other players have to look for the horseshoes and follow the trail to the treasure.

Decorate your own unicorn

Ask an adult to draw a big outline of a unicorn on a piece of paper. Use pens, paints or crayons and lots of glitter to decorate your unicorn. Glue on little pieces of wool or ribbon, or strips of coloured paper for a mane and tail. Choose a name for your unicorn and write it underneath. Then you can display it on your wall.

Make a unicorn hair braid

If you have long hair – or a doll with long hair – try making a unicorn braid. Brush all your hair over one shoulder and divide it into two strands. Twist each strand in opposite directions as you twist them around one another to make a rope. Fasten at the bottom with an elastic hair band. It looks just like a unicorn's horn!